I0210730

ARCHANGELOLOGY
BARACHIEL
HEAVENLY
BLESSINGS

IF YOU CALL THEM THEY WILL COME

KIM CALDWELL

Archangelology LLC

A Division of Archangelology LLC

https://archangelology.com

Copyright © 2020 by Kim Caldwell

All rights reserved.

No part of this book may be reproduced in any form or by any electronic or mechanical means, including information storage and retrieval systems, without written permission from the author, except for the use of brief quotations in a book review.

This publication is designed to provide competent and reliable information regarding the subject matter covered. However, it is sold with the understanding that the author and publisher are not engaged in rendering medical and healthcare or any advice. Archangelology LLC, Together Publishing and all offerings are for entertainment purpose only. If you need medical, financial or any kind of help please consult a qualified professional.

Introduction Editing and enhancement Rachel Caldwell

Book Editing Grammarly

ISBN: 978-1-947284-27-2

Book Cover Picture Nicola Zalewski

Cover design Kim Caldwell

❀ Created with Vellum

1

ABOUT THE SERIES

"Logic will get you from point A to B. Imagination will take you everywhere."-- Einstein

∾

This Archangelology book and the entire series aim to lift the reader one step at a time. You may read this piece anytime you desire Upliftment and want to feel good now, never underestimate the power of feeling good for creating more of what you want.

Choose this or any of the other Archangelology Books or Matching Audios to read or listen to for at least 44 nights and raise your vibration consistently for an Uplifted Feeling and Life.

This piece is one of a series of Angelic Upgrade books that fill you with Divine Angelic codes. Angelic laws are based on love and light and thus, operate for free-will, so we must call and ask the Archangels for help.

When working with your book relax, take deep breaths and ground to Mother Earth. Focus on Intentions for whatever it is your heart desires that are for the highest good of all involved. Intentions for these energies that we can not see but feel when we are ready. There are those that believe The Archangels are the Ones that make Law of Attraction Work.

This series of books take on a life of its own as the Archangels move and play from book to book, creating a Delicious Alchemy. Each book becomes an instrument in this Celestial Symphony for a more fulfilling life. Many of the Archangel books also carry and infuse the Violet Flame and Divine Connection to Mother Earth for a transformational experience.

Each book has a matching meditation audio available for your listening pleasure at https://archangelology.com. Please visit our site for your gifts. The book and the audio have similar wording, yet according to the Angels, they Upgrade us differently. Each medium has a unique experience, energetically Upgrading us in distinct ways. Each time you read or hear an Archangel Upgrade, a new dimension is added or adjusted for your benefit.

Become interactive with your book; when inspired, read the words aloud, and let them roll over you, feeling the love and magic that the Angels radiate. When inspired create your own rituals; there is no right or wrong way. As you play with the rock stars of the Celestial realm, you can expect your life to become more heavenly, more peaceful.

You may Notice Many Words are Uniquely Capitalized throughout this series; this is yet another way the Angels infuse us. When you see this try to feel that word or phrase; sensing the depth of its Intensity of Pure Divine Light throughout your Being.

The Archangel Energy is neither male

nor female. This gender fluidity is made clear in this series by the use of the word they or he/she speak to convey a non-gender energy that shifts roles to uplift and nurture you. The upgrades happen in Divine Time, and there is no schedule. There is no competition. There is no rush. Wherever you are in the process is perfect.

A word about the length of this book. "Less is more." This Series of books is the result of decades of study in the art of Law of Attraction, Angelic knowing and energy healing, condensed here for you in a format that will shift and benefit the reader. If you found your way here, you can expect miracles. As Einstein said, "There are only two ways to live your life. One is as though nothing is a miracle. The other is as though everything is a miracle." The matching audio to this book is 44 minutes, so working with that is always an option.

Both Neville Goddard and Albert Einstein stated that our imagination is the creative force. Goddard went so far as to imply that our imagination is the God/dess Energy. I mention this to you because as you read these words with much more than your eyes, let your imagination run wild with vivid pictures of the love the magical Archangels have for you and of your adventures together. Enjoy.

2

ABOUT ARCHANGEL BARACHIEL

≈

Barachiel Brings Great Blessings To Our Lives by helping Us Focus on the Blessings that already Exist, thus Multiplying them.

Barachiels' message is to Feel our Blessings to experience more Heaven on Earth.

When Archangel Barachiel made themselves known to me a year or so ago, I was delighted. What would Barachiel bring to the Archangelology Series that was not already here? If you have been following this Uplifting book and audio series, you know that each Archangel brings Unique and

Powerful gifts: the Archangel Alchemy— if you are new to the series, Welcome.

So in Floats, Archangel Barachiel in all their Majestic Angelic Glory blowing their Horn for Blessings. Barachiel reminds us that if times feel challenging, there are so many gifts to Be grateful and feel Blessed.

We can Breathe and get the "presence" of mind to take a moment or more to Count our Blessings and remember that All Is Well. We can do this, and the Archangels want to help us. Barachiel wants to help us.

Og Mandino reminded us in his classic book, "The God Memorandum" that your eyes to read or ears to hear this are great cause for Celebration.

I found The God Memorandum well over a decade ago and dutifully read it for 100 nights in a row, as Og suggested. At that time, the struggles were overwhelming, and reading a small book for 30 minutes or so a night seemed like a small price to pay for the freedom it gave.

Interestingly enough, when Archangel Barachiel's book came, I realized that each book in the Archangelology series could be read in about 30 to 44 minutes.

In the footsteps of Og Mandino, we will remember that reading an Uplifting short book for a prescribed number of nights will Create Positive Shifts.

44 Nights of reading this Beloved Blessings Infusion with Barachiel is suggested to receive maximum benefits. If this is not the time for that, enjoy this small book for daily contemplation and Focus on Blessings and more. Our Daily habits make us who we are.

As you Focus on Love and all your Blessings Daily, the Magic happens.

After completing the first 44 nights with Barachiel, you may get creative with your reading schedules and choose different Archangel books each night.

The great Wayne Dyer taught that "you don't have to change your life, just your mind." I like to imagine that Wayne is one of our Angels. He was undoubtedly an Earth Angel. Thank you, Wayne.

Playing with the Archangelology Series will Uplift your Mind and thus enhance your life. Every day with the Archangels is a gift.

Barachiel reminds us that we are never alone. You have such a Loving, unimaginably huge host of Angels and Benevolent Beings surrounding and protecting you now. It is the Archangels fondest wish to remind you to Celebrate the Love that is for and all around you from your Archangels.

You are an Earth Angel.

Just by Your very Existence, Love and Light anchors on our Divine Goddess Mother Earth. You are so Worthy. Please understand what a vital role You play here and Own that. There is no need to question your value ever again; you are a Divine Earth Angel.

The Archangels send beams of Love and Light to you on such a regular basis, and all you need do is Be Open to Receive.

When you think it is your Imagination as you hear Loving Messages from your Archangels, remember this--Neville Goddard and Albert Einstein said that Imagination is the Creative Force. Goddard went so far as to imply Imagination is the God/dess Energy. So as you hear your Archangels encouraging and

Loving you-- know how Loved and appreciated you are.

If times feel hard, pick an Archangel and Connect.

In your book, you will find three identical sections that are a Call for Divine Imagination Time with Archangel Barachiel. These sections are highlighted with eight little stars. This is when you will relax and breathe and paint Magnificent Mind Pictures of you and your Archangels that Feel wonderful. Barachiel will help you Bring Heaven to Earth with this practice. Be patient with yourself and allow this skillset over the next 44 days. Let this be an extraordinary delicious time for just you and your Archangel.

Call Archangels and simmer in Angelic Love, Protection, Abundance, and more, just waiting for you.

If you call them, they will come.

I send you peace and blessings, Kim Caldwell. Creator of the Archangelology Book and Meditation Audio Series

3

ARCHANGEL BARACHIEL

~

A rchangelology Archangel Barachiel Heavenly Blessings. Take a deep, refreshing breath. Archangel Barachiel has come to us, at this time, so they may remind us, "Spark" Us, help us to see and feel and experience all the Blessings, all the gifts that Heaven is bestowing upon Mother Earth and Us at this moment. Deep, Refreshing Breath.

Archangel Barachiel and the Archangels want you to know that we can experience Heaven on Earth any Moment we choose to. Deep, Aligning Breath. And Barachiel wants you to remember all the unseen help that surrounds you, that Loves you, that wants to bring Heaven on Earth to you every day. Deep, Enlivening Breath. All we have to do is Call.

Say with me now, "Archangel Barachiel, please come with me. Be with me and remind me how to Ignite my Heaven on Earth." Deep Supported Breath. Feel the Joy and Bliss as the Magnificient Benevolent Barachiel gently floats to land right in front of you. Yes, Feel them, see them. See them with your Heart, yes, Feel that Magnificent Celestial Energy all around You. Yes, Deep Focusing Breath.

As Barachiel takes your hand and lets you know that you're on a first-name basis, when you need them, call "Barachiel, Barachiel, Barachiel." Deep, Magnetic Breath. Three times if you like, and Barachiel will appear before you, around you in any environment you choose. They want you to know how powerful you are. They want you to feel your Confidence, your Divine gifts, and your ability to communicate with unseen Benevolent Forces that are here on the Earth Plane for you now.

Now, Barachiel knows what you are thinking because humans and Archangels communicate telepathically. And Barachiel answers. Yes, it is that simple-- You call, and Barachiel will come. Barachiel will shift the environment around you to that of Heaven on Earth. Barachiel lets you know that when you Call them and Together, Together, the master "Switchword," you Ignite everything around you with Golden Glimmering Light. Deep Blissful Breath. And with White Diamond Light. Yes. And the most beautiful Iridescent Light you can imagine. As you call Barachiel and all of this beautiful, delicious Light fills your environment, and your Being, Magic Blessings occur. A shift occurs, and Barachiel wants you to understand that you step back into your Power as an Earth Angel as this Blessing Happens.

****

Archangel Barachiel wants to "Sparkle" Your Life with Blessings and Bring you more Heaven on Earth. Take a moment to Breathe in all the Blessings you feel with your Vivid Imagination you are Activating Now. Allow yourself to go into Divine Appreciation for any Blessings that come to mind. No pressure; Connect with Divine Intelligence and Allow what comes. This may take practice, and You Can Do It. Archangel Barachiel is helping you, have Faith.

See in your Minds Eye as Barachiel Carresses You with Golden Light all over and Relax into this Angelic Love. Relax as Golden Light tingles and Ignites Your Blessings. Allow Your Imagination to Create Beautiful Mind Pictures of Blessings that make you Smile and are for the Highest Good. Do this as long as you like and feel Barbie Doll, Toy Car, good for a few Magnificent Moments. Allow your Childlike Enthusiasm. Enjoy this moment. It is all you and your Archangel. Say with me Now, "Something Magnificent is Happening." and pump your fist with Joy and Excitement. Feel the Excitement. Feel the Joy.

****

Barachiel wants to remind you that time is just an illusion on the Earth Plane and that they will Be playing with you to remember and learn how to collapse non-beneficial timelines. There are many timelines going on at once, and as we focus and feel our way--

we move to, from, and around different time-lines. Barachiel is here now to help us step into our Angelic Superpowers to collapse timelines that are not serving any longer. Deep Brilliant Breath. Moving our Vibration Up moves us to more desired timelines. So Up Up, we go with Barachiel.

One of the ways we can assist Barachiel in this play is to focus on our Blessings. Baruch is another word for Blessed. Barachiel, Baruch, Blessings.

As we blend our Powerful Imagination, the Creative Force, with our Blessings, the Magic starts to happen, yes. As we infuse Blessings into our Energetic Body with the help of Archangel Barachiel for the highest good, we begin to remember. We remember who we truly are; we start to remember that we are Spirits, Eternal, Ethereal Beings who have chosen a temporal human experience. Chosen to be here at this time to help bring Heaven to Earth. And Barachiel comes now to bring Unseen Benevelont forces to stand with us, before us, to stand around us, to support us in this Mighty Active Earth Angel Energy. Deep, Refreshing Breath.

Now, Archangel Barachiel wants you to get so comfy and so relaxed. Barachiel wants to remind you that deep in the place of Stillness, Sweet Peaceful Breath, lies Quietness with Immense Power and Wisdom. That one of our Superpowers is the ability to go there Now

and Now and Now. That place Deep Within that is a Universe where so many aspects of Ourselves exist just waiting, just waiting for us to Connect. These are Genius aspects; these are aspects of Divine Sweet Love. These are aspects of Archangels and Enlightened Masters, who are You, A Divine Blessed Magnificent Being.

In the Quietness, in the Stillness, of the soul is a Deep Love and Connection, which Archangel Barachiel helps us Know.

Barachiel holds your hand and asks if you are ready to travel there now, through a wormhole, through a portal, to a place of the utmost Love. To a place where the Heart Energy Leads. Deep, Loving Breath. Feel Barachiel now in your Heart Center. See Glorious Glowing Golden Light in Your Heart Area, feel the tingling and warmth.

Your safe; Barachiel is holding your hand, and they understand this may be new to you. They want you to relax and know that all is in Divine Order. This Loving Light Intends to relax and allow you to connect with your Archangels more often with more Ease and bring Peace and Vitality.

As you go into the Heart space, feel the warmth, feel the Divine Golden Light, and feel the Power. Barachiel wants you to understand that when humans come from this Heart Space, they become Infinitely more Powerful with Love. As we learn to Create From this Divine Heart Space versus the mind, life becomes more.

Watch as Golden Sacred Geometry moves all around you with Barachiel; yes, feel it. See the Shimmering Sacred Geometry moving all around you in a circle; at times, it is a Lively Rose-Gold Light. Barachiel smiles at you and watches as you feel Youthful as your childlike innocence "Sparks," and you start to feel how Empowering this Love; this Love Energy is for you.

Barachiel lets you know that during dark times when humans closed off their hearts for their own good and protection, for their learning, for what would ultimately lead to this moment, it was a hard time. And now, as Barachiel and the other Archangels help us to heal and Bless and Open our Hearts to handle more "Love Light" to share more "Love Light" to Create with more "Love Light"-- Well, it is time. Deep Loving Breath.

Notice as the Rose Gold Sacred Geometry around you creates beautiful, shimmering Opalescent Hearts. Yes, feel the Sacred Geometry, and you relax now.

A Charismatic Being starts to walk Up-- Sanat Kumara, and the Energy becomes Magnetized-- Sparkling. You feel as this Benevolent Enlightened Master makes his way to you. His eyes fill with the Sweetest of Love, and he lifts his Hand and Places it on your Heart Area while you are in your Heart Space. Archangel Barachiel stands Behind you, Supporting you, Loving you, and these two Magnificent Benevolent Beings start to Infuse your Heart, your Universe, your World, your Energetic Body with Cosmic Sweet Love. Deep Magnificent Breath. Now, feel as this Energetic Love Permeates every

Cell, every Thought, every Belief, every Lifetime, every Dimension with Divine Blessings. Deep Divine Breath, every one of your Higher Self Aspects, any parts of you that would like a little Sparkle. Yes, deeply Sparkling, Breath.

Sanat telepathically lets you know how much you are Loved, how perfect you are as you feel yourself start to float, drift as Sanat Kumara, and Archangel Barachiel each take one of your hands. Now the three of you begin floating, start flowing, out into the Universe, Yes, and you begin to feel what a Blessed Experience and moment this is. And you start to remember that you called for this, that you have asked for more Love and Peace, and to remember all the Blessings that have been bestowed upon you. As you feel all these Divine "Sparks" of Light and Love around you, all through you, as you taste the colors, the Watermelon Pink, the Lemon Gold, and as you are "Sparked" by Archangel Barachiel and Sanat Kumara to remember the Power of your Imagination. To Instill you with this gift and this ability to go into deep states of understanding your Blessings Now.

To be able to call for this feeling place anytime you choose. To Emerge from any heavy energies and move Up, Up, Up into the Celestial Blessings. Deep Angel Breath.

Yes, Now feel a tingling at your back, and start to remember to Activate Your Divine Angel Wings. Yes, Deep Angelic Breath. Barachiel smiles at you. Sanat smilies as Well, as you see yourself as the most Magnificent Angelic Superpower Being that you can imagine. See yourself now surrounded by Angelic Unseen Beneficial Forces that support you. Feel your Freedom. Experience your Wings Tingle and Shimmer a little. Watch Opalescent color on the fringe of your Wings. Now, your Wings are Strong and Powerful, and they are Etheric. So you know they are there. You know they are there.

Archangel Barachiel reminds you that when you want to create a Magical cloak of invisibility, you can draw your Angel Wings around yourself, yes, and Be Secret. When you feel that you want to blend in and send Love, your Angel Wings can assist you in this and help you to feel even safer and even more powerful and Divine. You will play with your Angel Wings, and Archangel Barachiel wants to let you know that they will help you. That you call Archangel Barachiel, and they will surround you with their Divine Beautiful Golden Light, and they will help you with your Magical Angel Wings.

With your Childlike Enthusiasm, you may Arise, Glow, Learn and Be the Powerful Earth Angel you planned to become when you came here to the Earth Plane. As you do this, you will more and more Easily Spread Light and Love, Yes, Deep Revitalizing Breaths.

We remember our Healthy Boundaries, and we Always stay True to Ourselves and do what feels best to Us, for the Highest Good. The Archangelology Michael and Violet Flame Books and Audios help with this and may want to Be combined here. Archangel Alchemy is so Divine. And the Archangels Love to play Together to help us.

In floats, the amazing Archangel Zadkiel. Zadkiel, the keeper of the Violet Flame. And Archangel Zadkiel wants to show you another process; anywhere you go, you may spread your Violet Flame like a carpet all over for thousands and thousands of miles. This Violet Flame will soothe and heal and clear any areas. You may want to spread this Violet Flame Carpet throughout your Whole home and then move it out into your neighborhood and then move it for thousands of miles above, below you, and in all directions, in a circle, around you, yes. This goes along with the Holographic Nature of the World in which we are playing. Archangel Barachiel wants to remind you that the Whole World is a screen and that with the Archangel help, with Sanat Kumara's help, with the use of the Violet Flame, we will Create the Holographic pictures and World that you feel great envisioning. And we do this from the Heart Center, remembering that the Heart Center is Infinitely more powerful and Magnetic than anything. Deep, Violet Breath.

****

Again, Archangel Barachiel wants to "Sparkle" Your Life with Blessings and Bring you more Heaven on Earth. Take a moment to Breathe in all the Blessings you feel with your Vivid Imagination you are Activating Now. Allow yourself to go into Divine Appreciation for any Blessings that come to mind. No pressure; Connect with Divine Intelligence and Allow what comes. This may take practice, and You Can Do It. Archangel Barachiel is helping you, have Faith.

See in your Minds Eye as Barachiel Carresses You with Golden Light all over and Relax into this Angelic Love. Relax as Golden Light tingles and Ignites Your Blessings. Allow Your Imagination to Create Beautiful Mind Pictures of Blessings that make you Smile and are for the Highest Good. Do this as long as you like and feel Barbie Doll, Toy Car, good for a few Magnificent Moments. Allow your Childlike Enthusiasm. Enjoy this moment. It is all you and your Archangel. Say with me Now, "Something Magnificent is Happening." and pump your fist with Joy and Excitement. Feel the Excitement. Feel the Joy.

****

Walk with Archangel Barachiel, Archangel Zadkiel, and Sanat Kumara Now onto a beautiful, refreshing land. Deep Refreshing Breath. As you walk through this Lush Green Field of Dreams, you notice the most Enchanting Flowers, Cosmic Flowers, you have ever experienced before. The colors Uplift and Transmute, colors so charming that your imagination gets more and more passionate, and you smile as you feel all these Energetic Flowers calling you. You feel so happy and enlivened, and you notice as you come upon a Magical Crystalline Structure. These Enchanting Crystals remind you of the size of the Stonehenge Boulders. And they are so "Sparkly," and you see the Light moving through them, and you feel Divine Sunlight streaming down and warming your body. You feel such a connection to these Magical, Mighty Crystals, and you notice as Beneficial, Crystalline Energy in your body slowly and comfortably Ignites — deep knowing Breath.

You notice a vast Amethyst crystal and the connection between you and this Amethyst. You experience the minute sparkling crystals in your body, moving fluid, liquid crystalline, Yes. And you feel this huge Amethyst crystal infusing your crystals in your Energetic Field, in your body, infusing you with Peace and Strength, Yes. Archangel Barachiel is right beside you, making you feel

Loved and Supported, guiding you in this adventure. And as you connect with this Amethyst Crystal, you feel Violet Flame swirling your throat chakra and helping to soothe this area of your body. Our throat area is an area that helps to clear out heavy emotions—deep, soothing Breath. The Violet Flame, Archangels, Sanat Kumara and Amethyst are releasing any lifetimes where things felt a little challenging--when we did not feel safe to speak. Archangel Barachiel telepathically lets you know that all those timelines are collapsing, Yes. Archangel Barachiel holds your hand as you feel a sigh of relief, yes take a big sigh now just let it go, yes. Barachiel and Sanat Kumara collapse those timelines and let you know that it is now safe. They also remind you that some-times the best thing to say is nothing and Activate your knowledge as to when to speak and when to stay silent. Remembering that sometimes "Silence is Golden" as more Golden Light shimmers around you and Barachiel Smiles their little knowing Smile ever so quietly.

Deep knowing Breath.

You see another Boulder Size Crystal, Sparkling Pink with Rose Gold Energy Shimmering; Archangel Barachiel explains that this is a "Rose-Star" Crystal Quartz. With this Rose-Star Quartz, feel the Love Activation of all the crystals in your Energetic body, your Heart, your lifetimes, with Love, the beautiful "Rose-Star" quartz, yes. All this Dynamic Love Energy moves through the microscopic crystals in your body; through your fluid crystalline body, yes. Deep, Tingling Breath. And your Heart-Chakra and this Rose-Star Quartz Crystal Connect, as you walk Up to the crystal and Embrace it, Yes. This Crystal Love Essence supports your Being, and Archangel Barachiel places their hand on your lower back. Experience this Infusion of Love, and watch as Sanat Kumara smiles at you with their eyes ablaze with Adoration. Take Deep Divine Breaths and feel this Infusion of Love. Yes, so wonderful, and you relax and smile as your Whole Energetic Body absorbs all this Devotion. Archangel Barachiel infuses you with the understanding that any Timelines where there is heartbreak are being collapsed Now. See as an endless row of Angel Wings covers the entire Timeline in both directions, and it gently dissolves away with Ease. You Move to the Exquisite Sacred Timelines of Love, where you can give Love, where your Heart is filled with an Infinite Supply of Love, where you have the beautiful Archangel Barachiel and Benevolent beings to support you in this Magical Ability.

There is one more boulder size crystal; it is iridescent and shimmers with Light. Archangel Barachiel lets you know that this is a Moonstone. You walk over to this Magnificent Moonstone Boulder, and it is so Captivating that you feel all of its Divine Energy Embracing you. It is Inspiring you with Happiness, with Joy, Yes, with Bliss, Yes. Instilling you with Divine Feminine and Divine Masculine energies Together. Deep Fulfilling Breath. You relax as the Energy from this Divine Moonstone Boulder starts to Radiate and Charge all the Liquid Crystalline Light in your body, as it moves through and flows with Ease. Ah, the Joy, take a Deep, Enlivening Breath. Yes, with Joy, and you now feel so Happy and so Blissful, that you might even Sing.

Archangel Barachiel explains that any Timelines where things were heavy and depressive are being collapsed now, and they are guiding you to more timelines with Happiness and Joy. Sing it. Sing the Joy. Sing the Bliss. Sing Your Love. Sing to your Archangels. Sing "All is Well, All is Well, All is Well With Barachiel. As many times as it feels good and anytime you want to Uplift, remember that All is Well With Barachiel.

See as Infinite Archangel Wings Fold over on this Timeline, collapsing it with Grace and Ease. Feel a sigh of relief as any heavy Energy Dissipates.

Barachiel reminds you to sing to them, and they will come to you, and they will help you Raise Your Vibration and Progress to the Timelines that are for your Highest Good, and brings you Love and Peace and great Joy. You may also enjoy working with Archangel Sandalphon in this Series as they help you Sing to your Angels for a closer connection.

You relax while Smiling as the Moon Angels drop down all around you with

Archangel Barachiel and Sanat Kumara and Archangel Zadkiel. These Magnificent Moon Angels Float Circling you. Raising your Spirits, Raising your Bliss, reminding you that all you have to do is call, and they will come. Yes, and you soak in all this Love, and all this Light as all these Benevolent Beings Shimmer your Crystalline Body, your Energetic Light Body, Mind, Spirit with this Divine Radiant Delicious Crystalline Diamond Light Energy, and you Sparkle like a Diamond. You Shine bright like a Diamond.

Archangel Barachiel explains that you are being Infused with the ability to Anchor Etheric Crystals in any Environment you feel guided. This is such a Blessing because as we lift and heal our environment, we feel better. This is a Miraculous gift, and with Patience and Practice, you will become a Master at it.

You may visualize Rose Quartz, Amethyst, Moon Stone, or your favorite crystal anchoring anywhere that needs a little more Love, Grounding, or a Boost, and no one needs to know you are doing this. Keeping things Secret gives the Soup time to

Simmer. Planting Energetic Crystals is just yet another of your Earth Angel Abilities to bring more Heaven to Earth. As you call Archangel Barachiel and any of the Archangels, you will become more Gifted at Anchoring Angelic Energies onto Mother Earth for the highest good.

****

Again, Archangel Barachiel wants to "Sparkle" Your Life with Blessings and Bring you more Heaven on Earth. Take a moment to Breathe in all the Blessings you feel with your Vivid Imagination you are Activating Now. Allow yourself to go into Divine Appreciation for any Blessings that come to mind. No pressure; connect with Divine Intelligence and Allow what comes. This may take practice, and You Can Do It. Archangel Barachiel is helping you, have Faith.

See in your Minds Eye as Barachiel Carresses You with Golden Light all over and Relax into this Angelic Love. Relax as Golden Light tingles and Ignites Your Blessings. Allow Your Imagination to Create Beautiful Mind Pictures of Blessings that make you Smile and are for the Highest Good. Do this as long as you like and feel Barbie Doll, Toy Car, good for a few Magnificent Moments. Allow your Childlike Enthusiasm. Enjoy this moment. It is all you and your Archangel. Say with me Now, "Something Magnificent is Happening." and pump your fist with Joy and Excitement. Feel the Excitement. Feel the Joy.

****

Thank you, Archangel Barachiel; thank you, Sanat Kumara; thank you, Archangel Zadkiel; thank you, Moon Angels, Thank you.

Archangel Bonus

Connecting with Archangels is a bit of a process, and there is never any rush. This energetic Upgrade and Exchange takes place in its own time. If you are new to the Series, you may want to ease into this Bonus. If you are an avid practicer of the Archangelology Series, you may want to jump right in on this Bonus. There is no right or wrong. Do what feels best, and you know. Also, some days may feel great to add this and some not—all good. The only rule with the Archangelology Series is to do it when it feels good and enjoy the Process.

We will thank each Archangel in this Series for all their help and Blessings they bestow upon us--thus aligning with the Archangel Blessings Energy.

Archangel Michael, Thank You for the Blessings you bring of Energetic Protection, Boundaries, and Cutting Cords.

Archangel Raphael, Thank You for the Blessings you bring of Abundance and Vitality.

Archangel Haniel, Thank You for the Blessings you bring of more Self Love, Loving Relationships, and Magic to my life.

Archangel Raziel, Thank You for bringing the Blessings of more Divine Wisdom in my life. Wisdom for Health, Love, Wealth, and More.

Archangel Camael, Thank You for bringing the Blessings of helping to Clear fear and feel more Courage in my life.

Archangel Uriel, Thank You for bringing the Great Blessings Of Peace to my Body, Mind, and Spirit.

Archangel Gabriel, Thank You for bringing the Blessings of more Creativity and Hope to my life. If I have Hope, I will make it.

Archangel Metatron, Thank You for bringing the Blessings of Well-Being and Sacred Geometry to my life. Your Golden Magical Energy Abounds.

Archangel Zadkiel, Thank You for bringing the Blessings of Forgiveness, the Violet Flame, and Your Violet Flame Dragons to my life.

Archangel Jophiel, Thank You for bringing the Blessings of Non-Judgement to my life to help me Glow with Youthful Radiant Energy.

Archangel Sandalphon, Thank You for bringing the Blessings of Harmony and helping me Sing to my Archangels, making me confident and closer to the Source Energy.

Sun Angels, Thank You for bringing the Blessings of More Power to anything needed at the moment.

Magnificent Moon Angels, thank you for bringing the Blessings of Magnetism for a happier life.

Archangel Orion, Thank You for bringing the Blessings of Cosmic Consciousness to my life during this unprecedented time in human evolution.

Thank You, Thank You, Thank You, Gorgeous Beautiful Archangels for all The Blessings You Bring to My life, and more.

4

SOMETHING MARVELOUS IS HAPPENING

One of my favorite Angelic games is to play, "Something Marvelous is happening." This idea came from a book called the Law and The Promise by Neville Goddard, and I have practiced this faithfully with great joy for years now. The benefits, along with a wonderful mood, are too numerous to mention. I will say it is well worth your time to play it if inspired.

It is super simple. You go to a time in your life where you were so happy, and you think about it and enjoy it for at least 30 seconds or so.

If, however, you can not find a wonderful time, you will ask the Archangels to help you make one Up. You will even bring your body into the process by pumping your fist and saying Yes, Yes, Yes, Something Marvelous is happening with Glee. You will probably want to be alone when you do that part--plus, keeping your ideas to yourself is always a good idea to give them time to come to fruition.

As this practice has evolved, I have added reminders to my phone to remind me to stop and get focused and create this exciting energy.

As Neville says, "It is the Feeling Place that creates."

The Universal Forces do not know if what you hold in your imagination is real or not; thus, this raises our Vibration and attracts more things we Love—like attracts like--so simple fun.

Play with it, have fun, and make it your own.

5

ANGELIC MANIFESTATION
JOURNAL BONUS

Writing down your Blessings with Archangel Barachiel on a daily or consistent basis is going to enhance your world. There has never been a better time to Focus on your Blessings with this Power.

Create more of the life you want with the Archangels as you explore and Focus with your Angelic Journal. If you are ready, let's set intentions now to make your Archangel Barachiel Book a Manifestation tool. It is said that humans have so many thoughts going on in our heads at once that it is hard for Angels and Spirit Guides to hear what we want help with. This is one of the many reasons it is so powerful to get very clear on what we desire and write it out in a designated journal for our Archangels. This way, they can understand our needs better and help us with our dreams and goals in Divine Time.

It has been proven that when we write things down, more of what we desire comes to us. Goals get accomplished, and things flow with more ease. Adding the Amazing Archangels to your journaling just makes the results that much stronger. As we set intentions for what we want and take the time to focus and write it down in our journal, unseen forces move on our behalf. We are going to enlist the help of this Divine Knowing with our Archangel book in an interactive way and turn our book into a manifestation tool. We are also going to play with our books like children and have some fun. Children are powerful creators, and we will take on some of their great habits for their creative value.

Focus and underline ideas you resonate with in your book and become immersed in Upliftment. There is a deeper connection as we become interactive with our Archangel books. We may get colored pens and underline areas of our book that feel important or special to us. We may want to draw pictures of desired blessings or anything that makes us feel good. We may want to mark different areas of our book with hearts, stars, or Angel wings. Get sticky tab notes, a personal favorite, and stick them to your favorite pages you want to return to often. In your journal section, place a sticky tab on an area you want to let the Angels know to help you write in and as a personal reminder. Let your Angelic interaction and intuition guide you with what feels best. Neville Goddard and Albert Einstein both explained that our imagination is a creative force and can bring great blessings to our lives. We will bring our imagination fully into our process now. You may want to add stickers to enhance pages. Place a beautiful angel or magic looking card in your book as a bookmark. Get creative and give your book some personal character. Putting clover or flowers in your book to press and dry, adds some powerful nature magic to your process. Roses are a great choice as they have the highest vibration of any flower. You may give lovely flowers as an offering to your Archangels as well. Giving back is always a beneficial activity.

Everyone has magical abilities. Some of us know this, and some do not. My point is all these ideas are simple and will work for anyone who puts forth an effort and has the faith to relax and let go so the Angels may do their work. Of course, anything we put out comes back to us, so we want to always include "for the highest good" in all requests.

In all my studies of magical herbs, cinnamon is found in many different traditions for enhancement of all things wanted and removing things not wanted. You may want to rub a dab of cinnamon mixed with a touch of olive oil on your journal in an intentional shape such as a heart for more love or the infinity symbol for more abundance. Then say to yourself, "I anoint my journal with success and happiness with the help of the Archangels." Anointment has been practiced for eons with much luck and advancement. Basil and Sage could just as easily be utilized. Anything that feels magical and speaks to you in your spice cabinet most likely has wonderful magical properties. Use these gifts of nature with intention and focus for a more joyous life. The idea is to create a magnet for all you desire that is for your highest good with your Archangel Journal.

You may want to underline ideas in colors that mean something to you. The sky is the limit, get creative and juicy with your book, knowing that amazing things are being created.

Next, we have dedicated pages that are waiting for you to fill them with your heart's desires that Barahciel will help you achieve as long as they are for the highest good. You may write anything you want in your Archangel Journal. There is no right or wrong way to do this. You may ask the Archangels to help you release things from your life, share your hopes and dreams, or ask questions. I ask my angels questions, patiently wait, and know they will lead me to the answer in Divine Time.

Be open and honest with your journaling and the Archangels understanding that the only ones who need to see your Angel Journal are you and your Angels. Keeping your wishes to yourself is very powerful for manifesting as well.

We have created categories for you, and of course, there will Be freestyle areas, so play with this and have fun. After you play with your journal, you may put it away in a sacred space knowing all is in Divine Order. Remember, magic works just in its own time and asking where the results are will only block things, so relax, have faith, and patience. Keep this dream book; you will be pleasantly surprised when you check on it at later dates. You may come back to read your Archangel book and add more to it at any time. Know that unseen beneficial forces are moving to help you now and forevermore. Play with and collect other Archangelology books and audios, remembering, "If you call them, they will come." Check out the Archangelology Archangel Journaling Book for more ideas on taking your Journaling Process to the next "celestial" level. The Archangels have tied this whole series Together for us in such a Divinely Intelligent way. Spend time in nature with your book, filling it with love, imagination, and Angelic magic for exponential results. You are a powerful creator and loved by all that is.

Write on the blank areas of your book and on the lined journal areas. Think outside of the box and let your kid like creative energies flow. Have fun, and add your own flair.

Please enjoy the process and expect wonderful things.

BLESSING JOURNALING

Write out all the Blessings you feel with this Magnificent Archangel by your side. See Golden Light blessings all in your Energy Field. I Am Blessed, and Archangel Barachiel stands by my side anytime I call them.

7

"BREATH-TAP" WITH BARACHIEL

I n the Archangelology Breath-Tap Book, we spend time with the Archangels Tapping for Vibrant Energy. Let us add a bit of this positive habit to our routine with Barachiel. Gently tap on the center of your chest while deeply breathing until you feel three Heavenly Blessings in your life to write down. Take as long as you need, and feels good. I will give you three to start with, and you may expound with your Blessings. "I have the eyes to read this. Archangels have my back. I have the lungs to take deep breaths."

After you list your Blessings, you may do

your Breath-Tap again until more Heavenly Blessings come. Keep this up as long as you feel good and get that Positive Chi flowing with Archangel Barachiel. Feel the Blessings Magnetizing as you Breath-Tap.

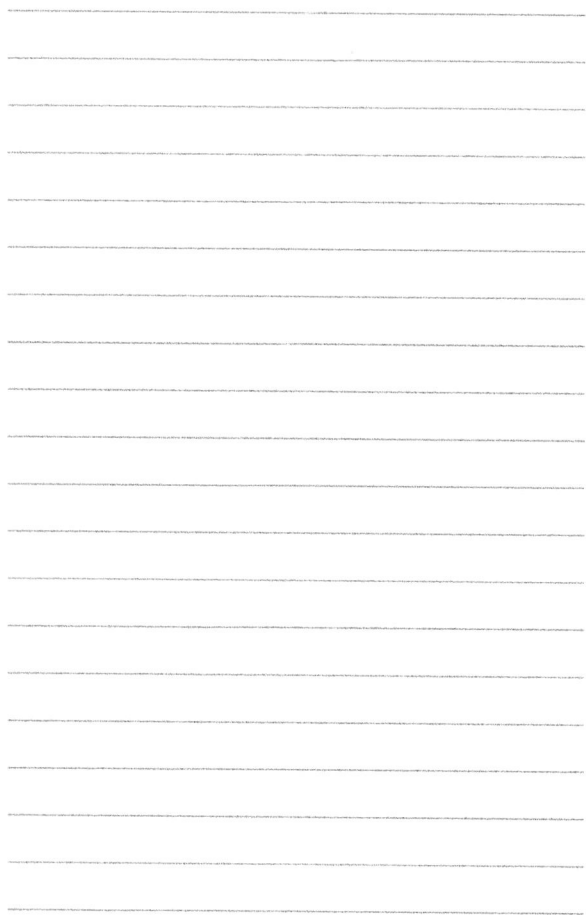

FINDING YOUR BLESSINGS MAGIC

Write out an Imagination Creation of how it would feel to find a Blessing chest with Archangel Barachiel. Hint, when you open it, it is filled with all the Love, Vitality, and precious Experiences of your dreams. And of course Golden Coins too if you like.

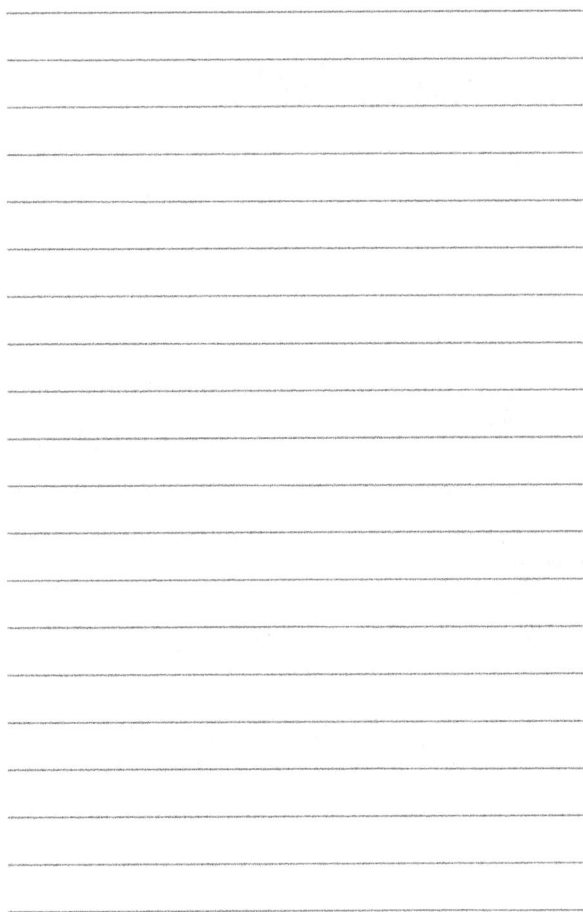

8

VITALITY WITH BARACHIEL

What does Vitality feel like to you? Let your imagination go wild with all the fantastic Vitality and Well-Being your Blessed With. Fly with Barachiel; the skies the limit. Do you radiate sparkles of Peace and Love? Archangel Metatron, the Archangel of Well-Being, wants to assist as the two create Archangel Alchemy all around you. Feel the tingles.

9

BARACHIEL BENEFICIAL TIMELINE ALIGNMENT

F ocus on Timelines you want to Align with more. Write out some desired timelines that feel great and lift your Vibration, Up, Up, while you think about them. Remember, Higher Vibrations means more desired Timelines. Timelines are, of course, New Thought, so play with it and make it you and your Archangels. The intention is, as always, to enjoy life more for the highest good.

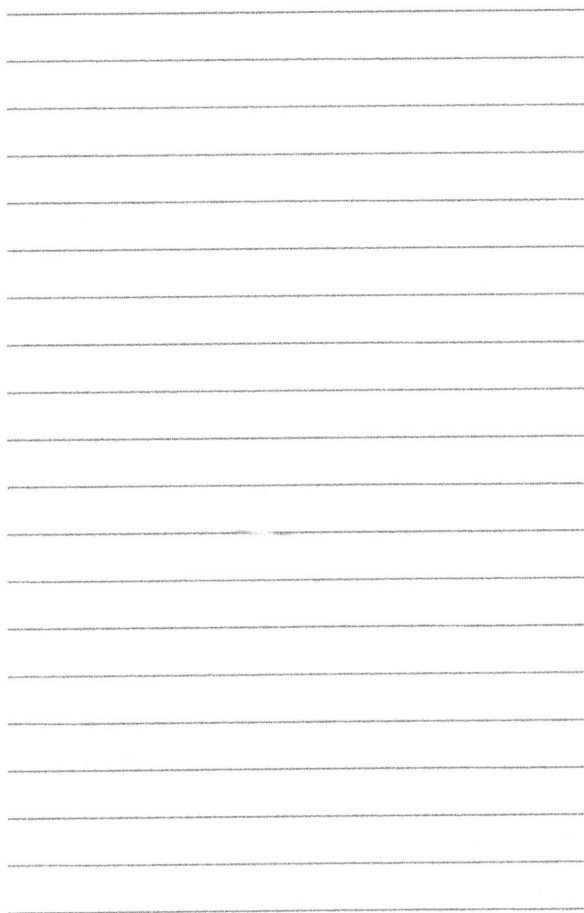

GOLDEN BARACHIEL BLESSINGS

How does it feel to Count Your Blessings Daily--to realize all the magic that the Angels have in store for you. Count is a Switchword which were created by James Mangan. For further exploration of Switchwords, check out the Activate Your Abundance Book and Audio Program by Kim Caldwell. Count is the Switchword to attract money. As in Count the coins. Journal about the fun it would be to Find Magical Golden Barachiel Coins. Find is the Switchword to Find a Fortune, Have Fun.

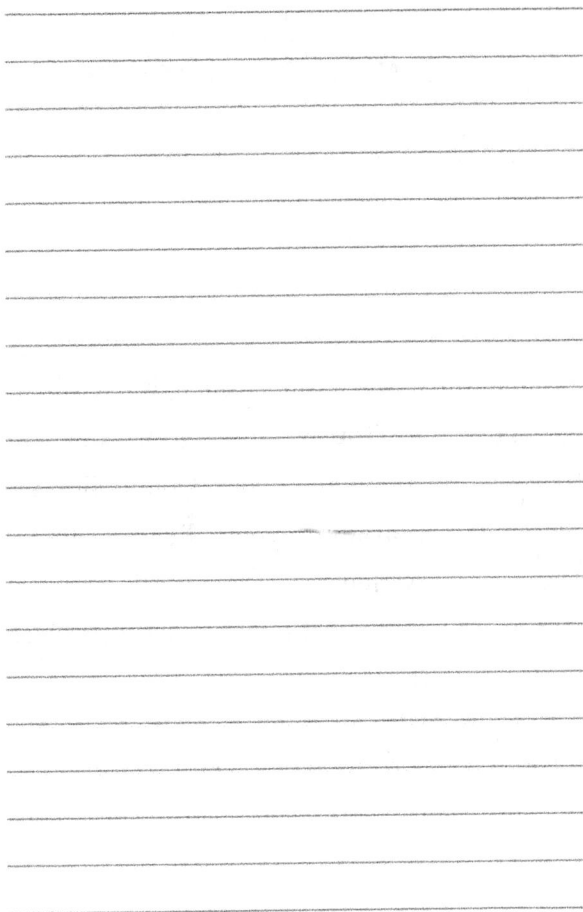

10

GOLDEN BARACHIEL TOUCH

I magine that you have the Golden Barachiel Touch. See your magical fingers Light Up as you direct Angelic Golden Blessings all-around your Energy Field. Describe how that feels. Expound, Expand, and Light Up. Up is the Switchword to move Up in a mood.

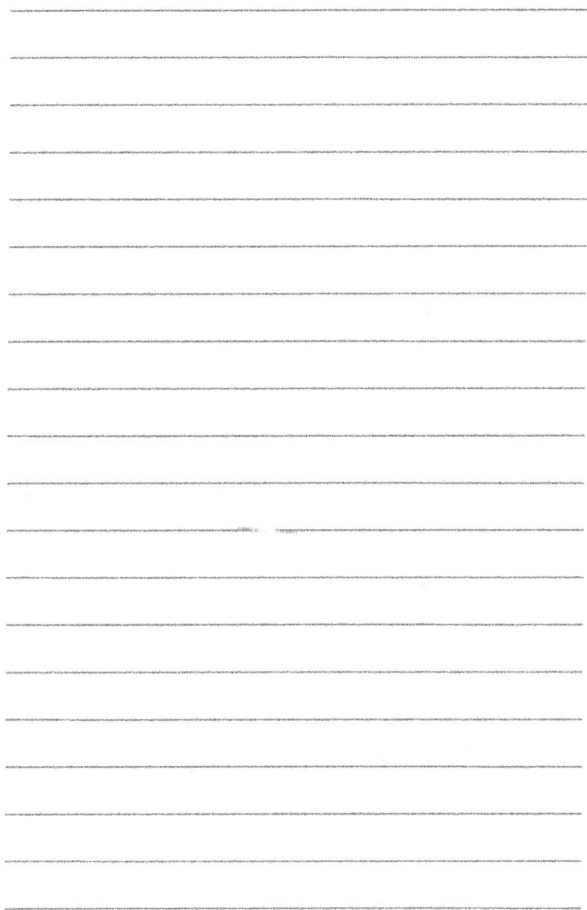

BE BLESSED

List all the Blessings Bestowed upon you. See them, smell them, feel them. Get great Bliss and Joy from them. Let Archangel Barachiel help you paint lovely mind pictures of all the Blessings, known and unknown, for the highest good. Be Blessed. Be is the Switchword to Be Healthy and more.

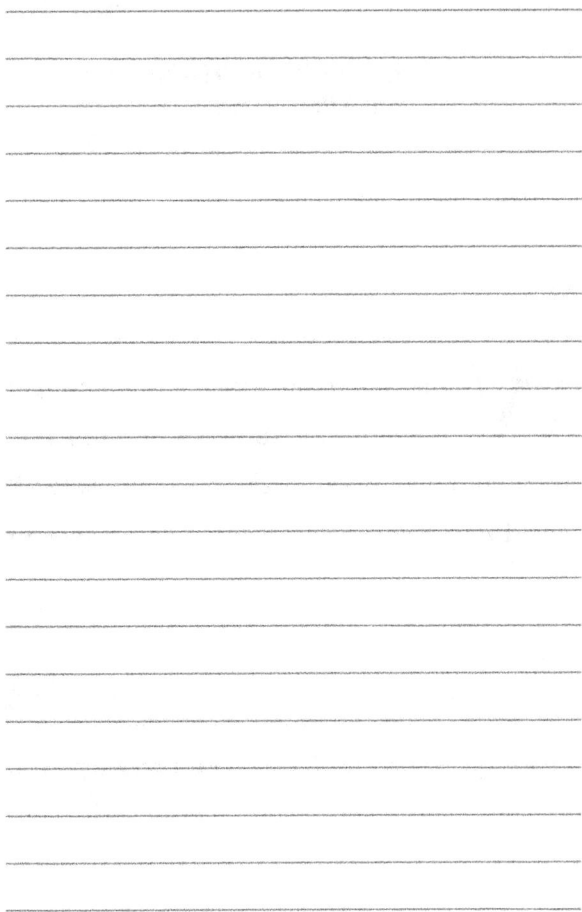

11

LOVE LETTER ARCHANGEL
BARACHIEL

W rite a Love letter to Archangel
Barachiel or someone in your life.
Let them know how much you appreciate all
they do for you.

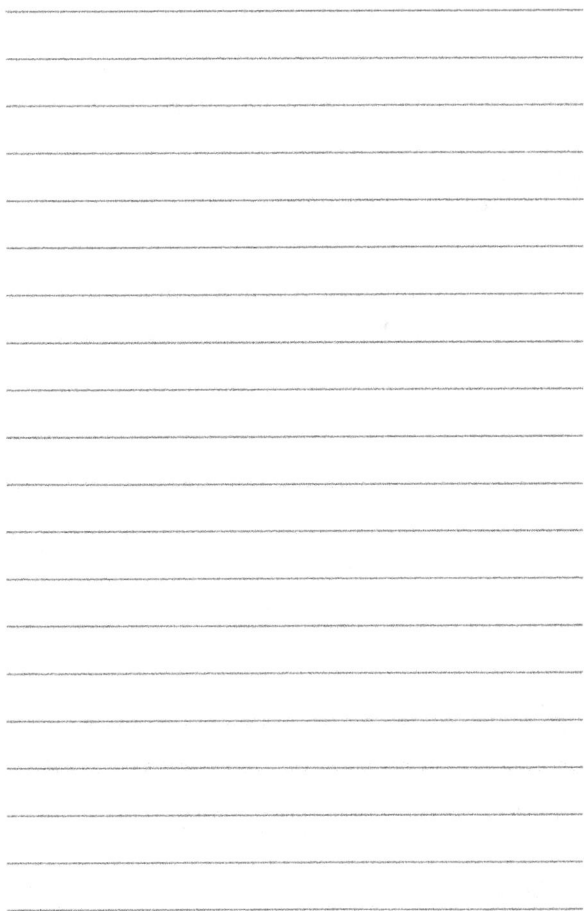

VIBRATIONAL NATURE LIFT

Spend some time in nature with your journal, listing all the Blessings you see and feel. Appreciate the immense Blessings the trees bring. Feel the Blessings of the Birds, Butterflies, and more. Take deep breaths enjoying the delicious fresh air. If the weather or conditions do not permit this, go there in your imagination now. Archangel Haniels' journey takes you to a magical beach. You may want to enjoy Haniels' book and or audio as well.

PLAY TIME WITH ARCHANGEL BARACHIEL

Remember how much fun play was as a child. If you can't think of a time, let the Archangels help you make one Up, and write all about it. Frolic and play with Archangel Barachiel and let them shine you with Blessings.

12

CREATIVE JOURNALING FOR A BLESSED LIFE

F ill these pages with any creative ideas that you desire your Archangels to help you line Up. Have fun. Get out your colored pens. Draw hearts filled with Violet Flame, beautiful landscapes, flowers, and anything that makes you smile.

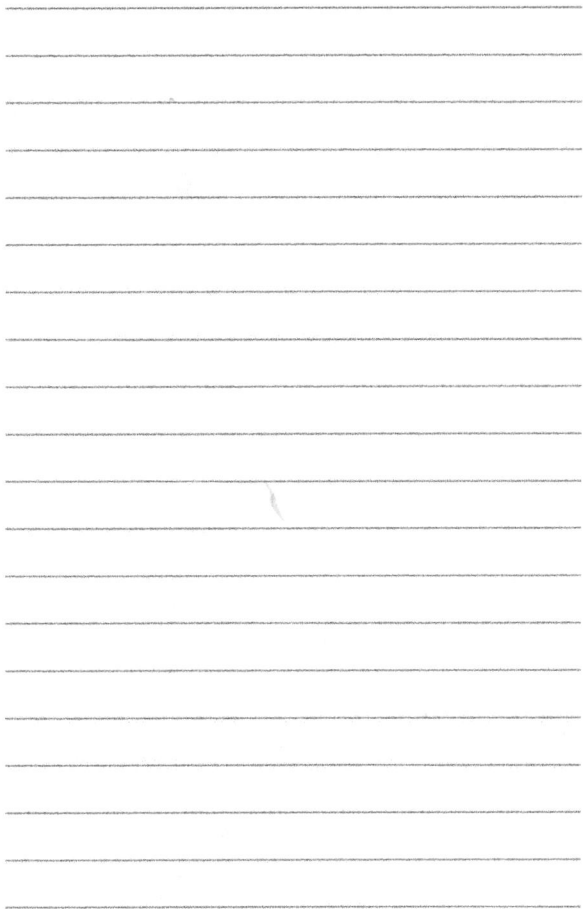

I AM LETTING MY CREATIVE
ENERGIES FLOW

F ill your journal with colorful drawings, symbols, and sacred geometry that attracts. Allow Archangel Barachiel to help you fill the page with Heavenly Blessings as Well.

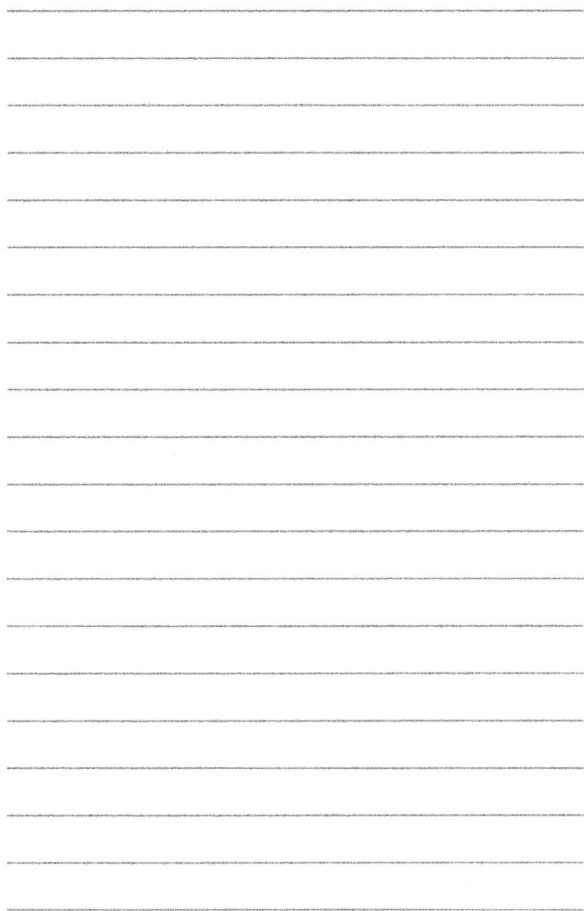

13

JOURNALING FOR NEW BLESSINGS

Ideas for New Blessings my Archangels help me bring to Life for the highest good. Let this evolve and grow for the highest good.

I AM FOCUSED ON MY BLESSINGS

Faith is the art of seeing the unseen. Ask Archangel Barachiel for help visualizing and playing with your imagination. Focus on all your Golden Blessings. See them floating around you and bring this to the page.

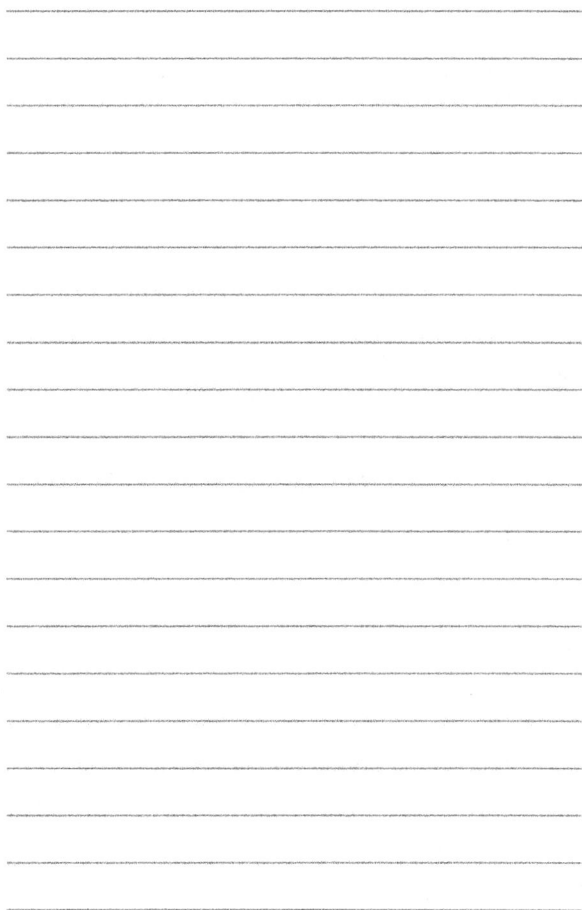

14

JOURNALING YOUR GRATITUDE

F ill these pages with the things you appreciate. Feel how abundantly blessed you are. The eyes to read this is cause for celebration.

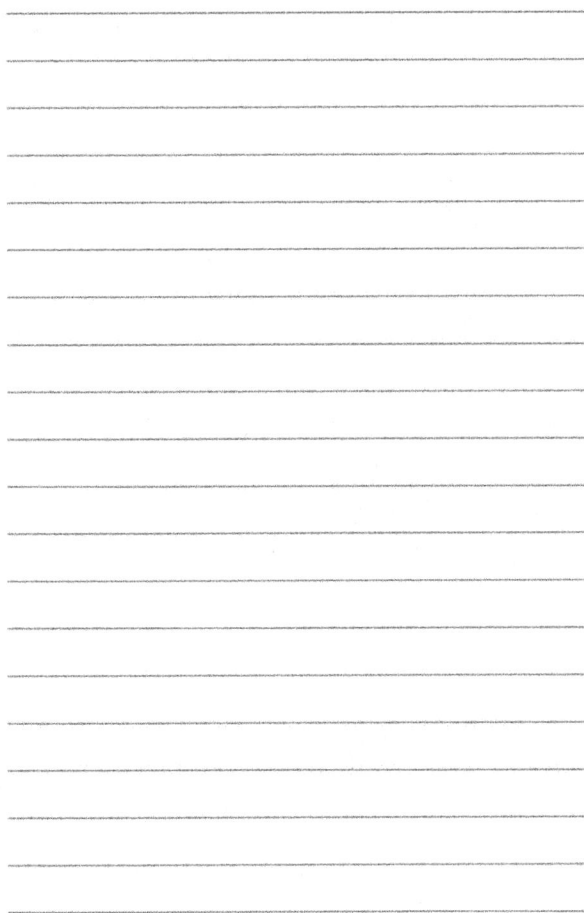

I AM A BLESSING MAGNET

Get in your playful energy and feel powerful. Remember things you loved doing as a child. Write out how it feels to be a Superhero who is Lucky and Attracts Blessings with Ease. What sort of costume do you wear? Have fun. This is just between you and your Archangels. Do your wings have gold or?

Enjoy your Imagination Creation.

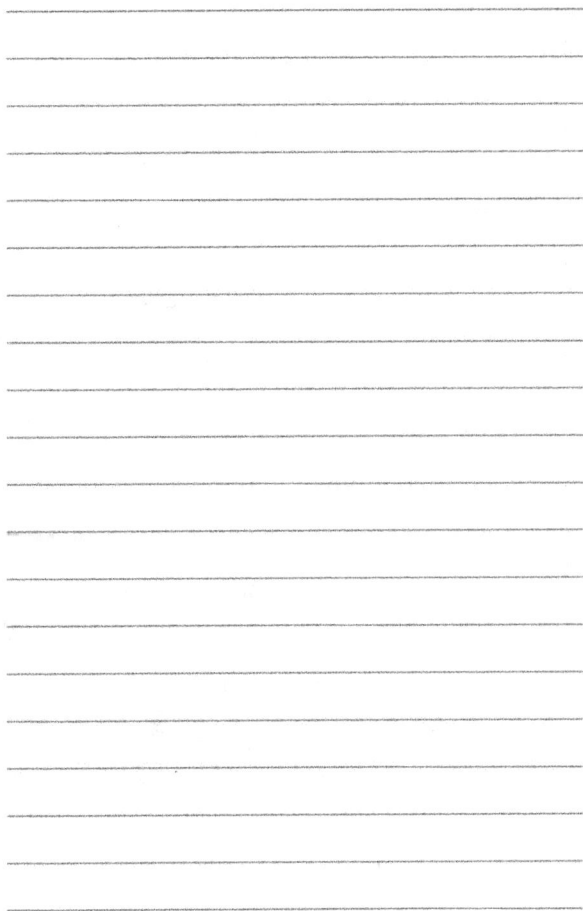

I AM A ABUNDANTLY BLESSED
FOREVER FREE

List your Blessings and things that make you feel Free, Blessed, Blissed, and more. Draw Pictures, the sky is the limit with the Archangels.

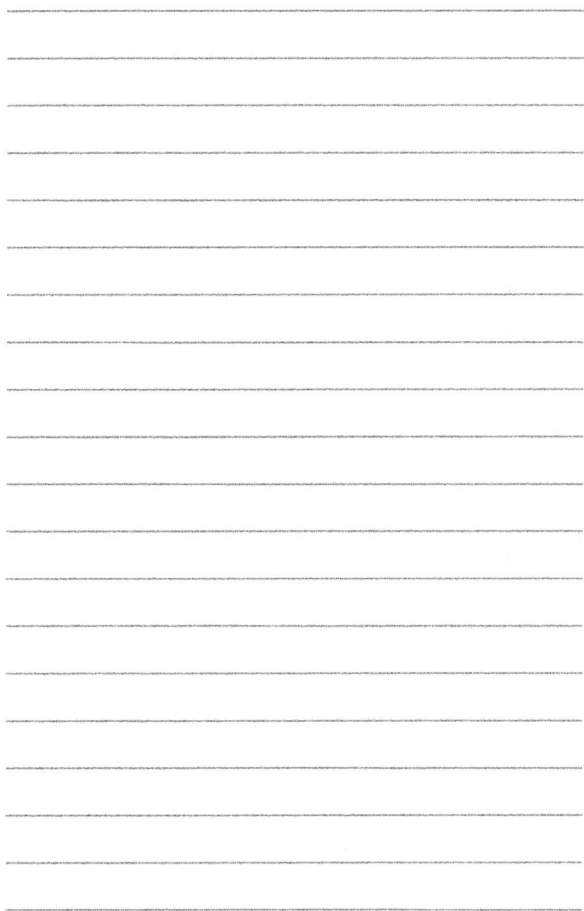

15

MY FAVORITE BLESSINGS

Take time, put on some of your favorite music, and write a list of things you love to do. List things you love to think about that make you feel bliss and proud of yourself. Feel how proud of you the Archangels are.

16

WRITE IT OUT

Accepting and making Peace with where we are is hugely helpful. In life, when things come up, that feel we have no control, a great tool is to "write it out." We will do this to write out all the anger, hurt and stressful feelings for "letting it go." As we let it go, we create space for more Peace. For this exercise, get a separate piece of paper that you will tear up once you finish writing out all the hurt and anger. This paper is for your eyes only, so say all the things you need to speak to the person or situation and do not hold back. Get it all out. Write and write till you feel a sigh of relief. This can take as long as you need it. Once you finish, you will tear the paper up and throw it away, or you may burn it in a safe place. Either way, the intention here is to let it go. If you need to do this process for more than one day, keep it up till you feel better. May this bring you Peace and Blessings or something better. Again, do not show this to anyone. This is for your relief and energetic shift. As you feel better, your world will too.

17

BLESSINGS

~

May the Divine Creative Force that Moves and Creates the Universes Bless and Enhance Every Wish You Ever Conceived that is for the Highest Good of All Involved. May Joy, Peace, and Purpose Be Yours all the Days of your Lives. Through All Time Space and Dimensions. So Mote it Be, and So It Is. I hope this book helps you in wonderful ways and radiates out to a gorgeous future for you and yours.

Kim

REFERENCES

~

Chaudhary Sufian. World of Archangels: How to Meet an Archangel. (Sufian Chaudhary 2012).

Damon Brand. The 72 Angels of Magick. (Damon Brand).

Esther and Jerry Hicks. The Essential Law of Attraction Collection. (Hay House).

James Mangan. The Secret of Perfect Living. (James Mangan)

Matias Flury. Downloads From The Nine: Awaken As You Read. (Matias Flury 2014)

Og Mandino. The God Memorandum. (Fell Publishers 1995).

MORE OFFERINGS

~

Visit https://archangelology.com to discover more Archangels and Super Power Saints

Each of the following books has a matching audio filled with healing music.

Archangelology Michael * Protection

Archangelology Raphael * Abundance

Archangelology Camael * Courage

Archangelology Gabriel * Hope

Archangelology Metatron * Well Being

Archangelology Uriel * Peace

Archangelology Haniel * Love

Archangelology Raziel * Wisdom

Archangelology Zadkiel * Forgiveness

Archangelology Jophiel * Glow

Archangelology Violet Flame * Oneness

Archangelology Sun Angels * Power

Archangelology Moon Angels *
Magnetism

Archangelology Sandalphon * Harmony

Archangelology Orion * Expansion

~

The items below come in book only

Archangelology * Archangel Journaling

Archangelology * Archangel
Breath-Tap Book

How Green Smoothies Saved My
Life Book

~

Activate Your Abundance Book and Audio
Program

~

The rest of the items below are available in Audio Format

Archangelology*Mary Magdalene*Feminine Divine Audio

Archangelology * Breath-Tap Super Power Saints Volume 1 Audio

Archangelology * Breath-Tap Super Power Saints Volume 2 Audio

Regeneration Meditations * Switchword Series with Solfeggio Frequencies audio

Radiating Divine Love * Switchword Series with Solfeggio Frequencies audio

Love Charm * Switchword Series with Solfeggio Frequencies audio

Dragon Sun Grounding Meditations * Cosmic Consciousness Series audios

Sweet Moon Sleep Meditation * Cosmic Consciousness Series

Enchanted Earth Sacred Geometry * Cosmic Consciousness Series audios

19

PLEASE WRITE A HELPFUL
REVIEW.

If you enjoyed Barachiel please give this Book a positive review so others may find it as well. And may blessings come back for your help.

Thank you so much.

Kim

www.ingramcontent.com/pod-product-compliance
Lightning Source LLC
Chambersburg PA
CBHW060414090426
42734CB00011B/2318